Storm Tracker

Allison Lassieur

Raintree

Chicago, Illinois

© 2007 Raintree
Published by Raintree,
A division of Reed Elsevier Inc.
Chicago, Illinois

Customer Service 888-363-4266

Visit our website at www.heinemannraintree.com

Designed by Michelle Lisseter and
Bridge Creative Services.
Picture research by Hannah Taylor and Rebecca
Sodergren.
Printed and bound in China by WKT
Company Limited.

1110 09 08 07
10 9 8 7 6 5 4 3 2 1

**Library of Congress Cataloging-in-
Publication Data**
Lassieur, Allison.
  Storm tracker / Allison Lassieur.
     p. cm.
  Includes bibliographical references and index.
  ISBN-13: 978-1-4109-2576-3 (library binding-
hardcover : alk. paper)
  ISBN-10: 1-4109-2576-5 (library binding-hardcover :
alk. paper)
  ISBN-13: 978-1-4109-2605-0 (pbk. : alk. paper)
  ISBN-10: 1-4109-2605-2 (pbk. : alk. paper)
  1. Storms--Observations--Juvenile literature. 2.
Hurricanes--Observations--Juvenile literature. I. Title.
  QC941.3.L37 2006
  551.64'52--dc22
                                    200600743

Acknowledgments
The author and publisher are grateful to the
following for permission to reproduce copyright
material: Corbis p. **19** (Raymond Gehman);
Corbis/Jim Reed Photography p. **24** (Mike Theiss);
Corbis/Reuters pp. **20–21**; EMPICS/AP/St. Petersburg
Times p. **25** (Douglas R. Clifford); Getty Images p. **11**
(Joe Raedle); Getty Images/Photodisc pp. **6–7, 14–15**;
NOAA p. **17, 18**; Rex Features/Keystone USA/BW/TS
pp. **22–23**; Science Photo Library pp. **4–5** (Jeff
Greenberg), p. **7** inset (Jim Reed), p. **13** (David Hay
Jones), p. **21** inset (Chris Sattlberger); Science Photo
Library/NASA p. **12, 27**.

Cover photograph of lightning storm, reproduced
with permission of Getty Images (Photodisc).

Illustrations by Bridge Creative Services.

The publishers would like to thank Nancy Harris and
Harold Pratt for their assistance in the preparation of
this book.

Contents

Some words are printed in bold, **like this**. You can find out what they mean on page 30. You can also look in the box at the bottom of the page where they first appear.

Weather Watchers

The skies grow dark. Black clouds roll in overhead. A storm is coming. How bad will it be?

Weather happens all the time, all over the world. Most of the time, the weather does not cause problems. But sometimes the weather gets dangerous. People need to know when dangerous weather is coming. Then they can get ready for the storm. Or they can get out of the way.

Storm trackers watch for dangerous weather. They **predict** when a storm will happen. They have many different ways of watching the weather. They use computers to watch the weather. They use airplanes to track storms. These tools help storm trackers know how dangerous a storm might be. Then they tell other people what kind of weather is coming.

predict   use special knowledge to tell something in advance

▼ *When dark clouds roll in, a storm usually follows.*

5

Powerful Weather

A storm can strike anytime and anywhere. It can happen during the day. It can strike at night. What makes storms happen? How does a small storm become big and dangerous?

Different natural forces cause a change in the weather. The Sun affects the weather. Air and **temperature** also affect the weather. Dangerous weather can happen when these things mix together in a certain way.

One type of dangerous weather is a **hurricane**. Hurricanes form when the air is warm and wet. The Sun heats the ocean. The warm ocean then heats the air above it. This warm air rises quickly. This is the first step in making a hurricane.

Strong storms

*Storms need **energy**. A hurricane needs warm, moist air. The warm air gives the hurricane energy. It helps the hurricane grow strong.*

energy	force or power
hurricane	storm that begins over warm water and has high winds, rain, thunder, and lightning
tornado	high-speed winds that spin around and form a funnel shape
temperature	measure of how hot or cold something is

A **tornado** is a very ▶ powerful storm. It forms over land. A tornado has winds that spin at high speeds. The winds form a funnel shape.

Lightning often strikes during a storm.

Where does violent weather happen?

Some types of storms happen only at certain times of year. Some types of storms happen only in certain places. Storm trackers know when to start watching for a storm. This is called the hurricane season. It is the time of year when hurricanes are most likely to hit.

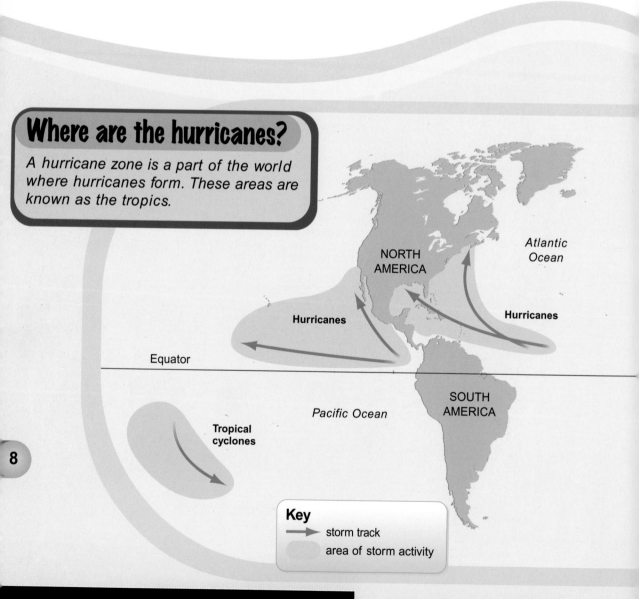

Where are the hurricanes?

A hurricane zone is a part of the world where hurricanes form. These areas are known as the tropics.

Atlantic Ocean

NORTH AMERICA

Hurricanes

Hurricanes

Equator

SOUTH AMERICA

Pacific Ocean

Tropical cyclones

Key

→ storm track

area of storm activity

tropical   from a warm, wet part of the world

Hurricanes form in **tropical** oceans. Tropical areas are warm. Hurricanes usually happen in the summer or early fall. This is when the water is warm enough for a hurricane to form. In the United States, hurricane season is from May to November.

Hurricanes also happen in other parts of the world. Other countries have different names for this type of storm. In Japan they are called typhoons. In Australia they are called tropical cyclones.

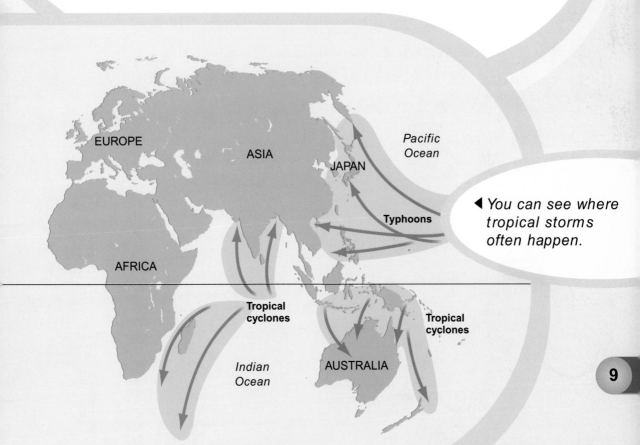

◀ You can see where tropical storms often happen.

Keeping an Eye on Storms

Many years ago, the best way to **predict** the weather was to look up. People watched for clues about changes in the weather. They looked at the clouds and wind. They watched how animals and plants acted. But these ways did not always work. Now we use tools such as computers and **radar** to predict the weather. Radar is a machine that takes special photographs of the sky. Computers and radar show where the rain clouds are.

The job of storm trackers is to gather information. They look at what the weather is like now. They measure the **temperature** and wind speeds. They study special maps. They talk to weather watchers in other parts of the world.

Storm trackers put together all this information. It helps them figure out what the weather will be like in the future. When a storm starts brewing, they will know about it.

Weather science

There is a special name for the science of watching the weather. It is called **meteorology**. *A* **meteorologist** *is a scientist who studies meteorology. Meteorologists watch the weather all the time. Tracking storms is part of their job.*

meteorologist   scientist who studies the weather
meteorology   science of watching the weather
radar   special machine that records distant objects

▼ Weather information is sent to computers from all around the world.

Weather-watching tools

Storm trackers use special tools to help them watch the weather. The most important tools are weather **satellites**. Satellites fly high above Earth. They take pictures of Earth below. Storm trackers look at these pictures. The pictures tell them where a storm might be forming.

Weather satellites ▼ take photographs of clouds from space. Computers on board also record temperatures.

satellite   object launched into space from Earth

Storm trackers use other weather-watching tools, too. They use **radar** to measure **temperature** and wind speeds. They also send weather balloons into the sky. These special balloons measure wind speed and temperature. Storm trackers use all this information to see where dangerous weather might be forming.

Tracking a Hurricane

Day 1
5:10 A.M.

Early one morning, storm trackers spot clouds over the ocean. They are near Africa (see map on page 9). A storm is beginning to form. It does not look like much at first. There are just a few clouds and some rain. But storm trackers are on the alert.

▲ This calendar will help you track the hurricane's progress.

They begin to watch this little storm very carefully. They know that the warm African waters are good for **hurricanes**. They know that many hurricanes start out here as thunderstorms. These storms have lightning and thunder.

The storm trackers quickly see that the signs are right for a hurricane. The wind patterns look right. **Temperature** and **pressure** readings also look right. A hurricane is possible. But will it happen?

A few hours later, the storm moves into the warmer ocean waters. This is not a good sign. But it is not a hurricane yet. So the storm trackers watch and wait.

pressure   force of something pressing down or against something else

▼ A hurricane is starting over the ocean. **Satellites** will help storm trackers follow its path.

Weak or strong?

It can take many days for a hurricane to form. Not every storm becomes a hurricane. A storm can weaken and die at any time.

From storm to hurricane

How does a thunderstorm turn into a **hurricane**? If the conditions are right, the storm will grow. More rain will fall. The winds will grow stronger. When the winds blow at 73 miles (117 kilometers) per hour, the storm is a hurricane.

The storm trackers check their **data**. Their tools tell them the storm is speeding up. The wind begins to spin around in a circle. The air is warm and moist. It is raining harder. The storm might turn into a hurricane.

But it is not time to worry yet. Storm trackers must watch this storm closely. The next few hours will be very important.

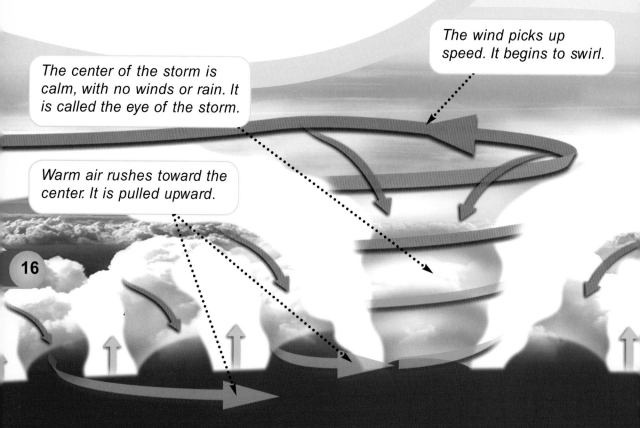

The wind picks up speed. It begins to swirl.

The center of the storm is calm, with no winds or rain. It is called the eye of the storm.

Warm air rushes toward the center. It is pulled upward.

16

▲ *This storm over the ocean is developing into a hurricane.*

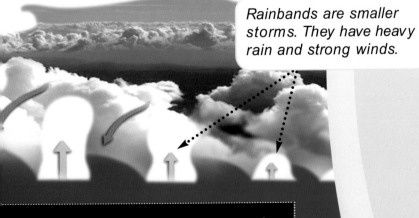

Key

→ warm air
→ cold air

Rainbands are smaller storms. They have heavy rain and strong winds.

data information measured by tools

Bigger and Stronger

The storm has now become a **hurricane**. It stretches across an area of 300 square miles (777 square kilometers) of ocean. But where will it hit land? And how much damage will it do?

The storm trackers must **predict** where the hurricane will make **landfall**. This is when it reaches land. They watch the path the hurricane has traveled. They use that information to figure out where it will go next.

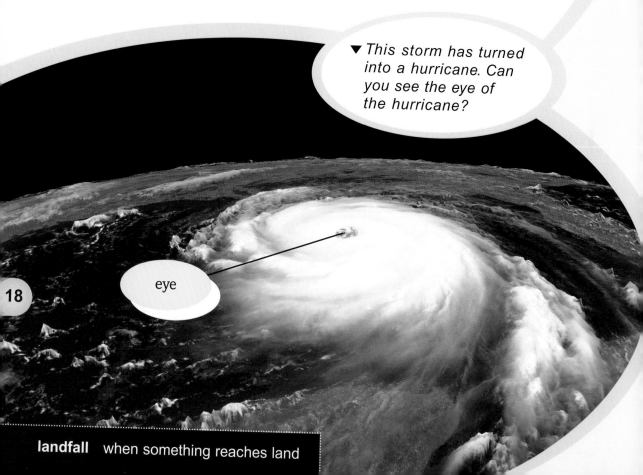

▼ This storm has turned into a hurricane. Can you see the eye of the hurricane?

eye

18

landfall   when something reaches land

Hurricanes travel at about 15 to 20 miles (24 to 32 kilometers) per hour. Storm trackers can figure out when the hurricane will reach land. But sometimes a hurricane will change speed. Some hurricanes change direction. The storm trackers will have to make the best guess they can.

▼ Hurricane Andrew did this damage. It was a category 5 storm. The hurricane hit south Florida and Louisiana in 1992.

Hurricane strength

Hurricanes are graded by strength. A category 1 storm is the weakest. Category 5 is the strongest.

Category	Damage
1	Very little damage.
2	Some trees might blow down.
3	Buildings are damaged. There may be some flooding.
4	Some buildings are destroyed. There is more flooding.
5	Many buildings are destroyed. There is a lot of flooding.

Hurricane Hunters

It is time to call the Hurricane Hunters. The Hurricane Hunters are special pilots who fly into **hurricanes**. Their job is to record **data** on a hurricane. Six people ride in a hurricane plane. Each person has a special job.

- The pilot flies the plane. The co-pilot helps the pilot fly the plane.
- The flight engineer makes sure the airplane is working properly.
- The **navigator** keeps the airplane going in the right direction.
- The flight **meteorologist** runs special weather computers.
- The **dropsonde** operator watches a special machine called a dropsonde.

Getting data

A dropsonde is a machine with a parachute attached. It is dropped out of the plane. The dropsonde records hurricane data as it falls all the way to the ocean.

dropsonde	machine that is dropped from a plane and records hurricane data in the air
navigator	person who steers or runs the controls

The Hurricane Hunters fly through the worst of the storm. It is a bumpy ride! Their computers record hurricane data. Then the Hurricane Hunters send the data to the storm tracker team.

▼ This airplane is part of a special unit called the Hurricane Hunters.

The Hurricane Hunters' ▶ plane must be very strong and sturdy.

Getting Out of the Way

The storm trackers know where the **hurricane** is going. Now it is time to tell people that the storm is on its way. The National Weather Service issues watches and warnings.

A hurricane watch is an alert that says a hurricane might come your way. A hurricane warning means that a hurricane is coming for sure. This gives people time to get ready for the coming storm.

Day 6
12:40 P.M.

Hurricane watch

Some things to do for a hurricane watch

If a hurricane watch is issued in your area:

- *Listen to the radio or television for information on the storm.*
- *Bring lawn furniture, trash cans, and potted plants indoors.*
- *Check that you have plenty of canned food, water, first aid supplies, and medicines.*

22

Hurricane warning

Some things to do for a hurricane warning

If a hurricane warning is issued in your area:

- Leave the area if local **officials** tell you to do so.

- If officials say you can stay, keep indoors and away from windows.

- Leave mobile homes.

- Stay away from floodwaters.

▲ These people are leaving town before the hurricane arrives.

23

Landfall!

The storm hits hard. This is a category 3 storm. It will cause a lot of damage. The National Weather Service has warned people of the coming **hurricane**. Some people left town. Others decided to stay.

The sky goes dark. It rains very hard. The wind blows at more than 100 miles (161 kilometers) per hour. Several mobile homes are destroyed. A few buildings are damaged. Trees and power lines fall over. The electricity goes out.

Hurricane Katrina blasts ▼ sand and rain along the coast of Mississippi.

Flooding

*A hurricane can cause a storm **surge**. A storm surge is a huge dome of water. It builds up as a hurricane moves over the ocean. The surge floods some areas.*

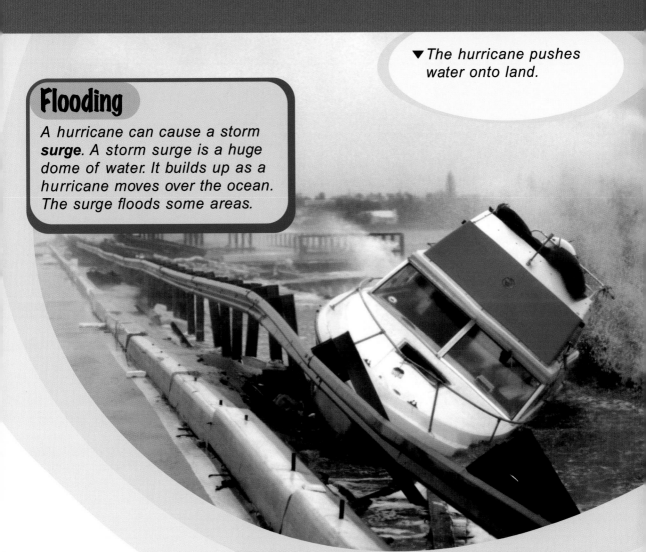

Two hours later, it is all over. People are amazed at how much damage the storm did. It will take a long time to clean up from the storm. But luckily, no one was hurt. The storm trackers gave plenty of warning that the storm was coming.

Moving inland

The **hurricane** does not stop moving. It moves farther inland. It brings more storms and rain as it goes. The storm hits many cities and towns.

The hurricane loses **energy** over land. The special conditions that made the hurricane are gone. The eye of the storm fills up with clouds. The hurricane becomes a rainstorm. Soon it will disappear.

Storm trackers watch the storm as it moves over land. They watch the amount of wind and rain it causes. They see when and where it dies out. This **data** will help them **predict** how future storms will act.

The storm tracker team's job is done for now. But another storm will come. It might be bigger. It might be smaller. When it starts, the storm trackers will be ready.

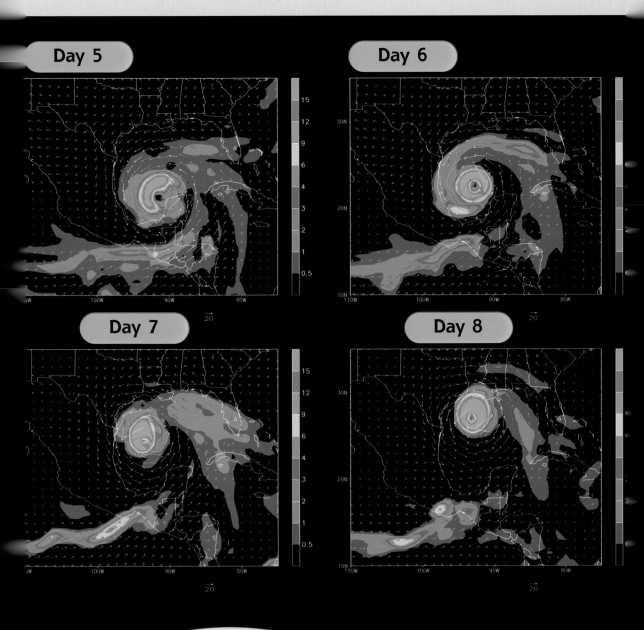

Day 5

Day 6

Day 7

Day 8

These pictures are made by ▲ a computer. Forecasters use computer models like these to predict the path and strength of a hurricane. The red areas show heavy rain. The blue areas show light rain.

Keeping Safe

Storms happen everywhere. Most storms are not very strong. When they are over, everything goes back to normal.

Sometimes a big storm comes along. Storm trackers watch for this to happen. They use many tools to help them **predict** how, when, and where the next big storm will happen. Then they warn everyone about the storm.

You can be ready if a big storm comes your way. Ask an adult to help you gather items for a storm safety kit.

Collect books, toys, and games to keep you busy if the electricity goes out.

Collect canned food. Don't forget the can opener!

If you have a cell phone, make sure it is charged.

Make sure there is plenty of drinking water.

Make sure you have a battery-powered radio, a flashlight, and extra batteries.

Pack a bag with some extra clothes.

Ask an adult to collect a first aid kit. If someone in your house takes medicine, make sure it is in the kit.

29

Glossary

data information measured by tools. Storm trackers collect data about storms.

dropsonde machine that is dropped from a plane and records hurricane data in the air. The Hurricane Hunters use a dropsonde to collect information about hurricanes.

energy force or power. A hurricane gets its energy from warm, moist air.

hurricane storm that begins over warm water and has high winds, rain, thunder, and lightning. A hurricane can cause damage when it hits land.

landfall when something reaches land. Storm trackers warn of a hurricane's landfall.

meteorologist scientist who studies the weather. Meteorologists study the path of hurricanes.

meteorology science of watching the weather. Meteorologists study the weather.

navigator person who steers or runs the controls. The navigator helps steer the plane.

official person in charge. In case of a hurricane, listen to your local officials.

predict use special knowledge to tell something in advance. Storm trackers can predict the path of a hurricane.

pressure force of something pressing down or against something else. Hurricanes can form when there is low pressure.

radar special machine that records distant objects. Radar helps storm trackers measure the strength of a hurricane.

satellite object launched into space from Earth. Storm trackers look at data from satellites.

surge push forward suddenly, with great power. Hurricane winds cause a storm surge to push onto land.

temperature measure of how hot or cold something is. Your parents may take your temperature if you feel sick.

tornado high-speed winds that spin around and form a funnel shape. A tornado can cause damage and injury.

tropical from a warm, wet part of the world. Hurricanes form in tropical areas.

Want to Know More?

Books to read

- Allen, Jean. *Hurricanes*. Capstone Press, 2000.

- Chambers, Catherine. *Hurricanes*. Chicago: Heinemann Library, 2001.

- Colson, Mary. *Turbulent Planet: Earth Erupts*. Chicago: Raintree, 2005.

- DK Publishing. *Hurricane and Tornado*. New York, NY: Dorling Kindersley, 2004.

- Sakany, Lois. *Hurricane Hunters and Tornado Chasers: Life in the Eye of the Storm*. New York, NY: Rosen Publishing Group, 2005.

Websites

- http://www.fema.gov/kids/ hurrtrac.htm
  This National Hurricane Center site is part of the National Weather Service. You can print out hurricane tracking maps or make your own.

- http://www.nationalgeographic.com/ forcesofnature/forces/hurricanes.html
  You can explore a hurricane and other forces of nature from this site. It includes maps, case studies, and 3-D images.

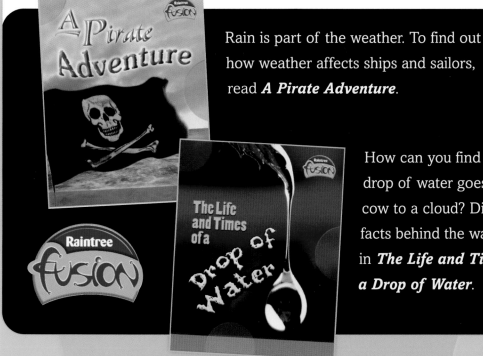

Rain is part of the weather. To find out how weather affects ships and sailors, read *A Pirate Adventure*.

How can you find out how a drop of water goes from a cow to a cloud? Discover the facts behind the water cycle in *The Life and Times of a Drop of Water*.

Index